CW01657670

STARTING OUT WITH THE NATIONAL CURRICULUM

An introduction to the National Curriculum and Religious Education

NCC
NATIONAL CURRICULUM COUNCIL

£5 rrp

ISBN: 1 872676 98 7

First published 1992

Printed in Great Britain

The National Curriculum Council is an exempt charity under the Charities Act 1960.

National Curriculum Council, Albion Wharf, 25 Skeldergate, York YO1 2XL.

Chairman: David L Pascall

CONTENTS

CONTENTS

FOREWORD

The National Curriculum lies at the heart of education in the 1990s. It is essential that all teachers in training understand the legal framework which now defines the foundation subjects and religious education if the objectives of the *Education Reform Act 1988* are to be met.

This book is a direct and practical response to this need. It aims to provide a concise and accurate introduction to the language, concepts and structure of the statutory curriculum for those who are new to it. It is not a substitute for the Orders, the non-statutory guidance or wider reading and discussion about the curriculum. Nor is it intended that the whole document should be read at one sitting. In most cases it is expected that tutors and mentors will be able to explain and clarify issues which arise from it. As the title implies, this book itself is only the starting point for thinking and discussion.

I am grateful for the close co-operation and help of CCW and SEAC in producing this book. I should also be interested to receive feedback from readers on how well you feel this book meets your needs.

David L Pascall
Chairman, National Curriculum Council
September 1992

INTRODUCTION

Schools of the 1990s will be very different from the schools in which today's student teachers were educated. The changes which affect the school curriculum are detailed elsewhere in this book, but the main forces for change have been:

- the introduction of a statutory curriculum and assessment;
- local management of schools (LMS), delegated school budgets and the autonomy these provide;
- the development of grant-maintained schools (GMS), City Technology Colleges (CTCs), and more open enrolment, offering greater parental choice and diversity of school;
- the greater participation, by law, of the governing body;
- the school development plan — and its approval by governors;
- teacher appraisal;
- the developing role of the national and local inspectorate.

The changes are enormous; their long-term nature inevitably means a continual process of evaluation and review. The cumulative effect of the changes will perhaps only be evident when the 5 year olds who started school in 1992 complete their compulsory schooling.

Teachers are crucially and properly involved in this process of evaluation and change. Although the content of the National Curriculum is laid down by law, how each subject is taught and how the curriculum is organised are matters for the headteacher, staff and governors of each school. It is the professional skill and creativity of individual teachers which will enable each pupil to gain maximum benefit from their experience of the National Curriculum.

Student, licensed and articled teachers have a major role to play in this process. They are the next generation of teachers on whom the continuing development of the National Curriculum will depend and they will need to be prepared for this.

The introduction of the National Curriculum has helped to clarify the essential knowledge, understanding and skills which new teachers need to acquire and develop during their initial training. These include:

- awareness of the statutory framework within which the National Curriculum functions;
- knowledge of National Curriculum subjects appropriate to the key stages for which they are being trained;
- an understanding of the broad nature of the whole curriculum and cross-curricular elements;
- insights into curriculum continuity and progression from ages 5 to 16;
- skills in curriculum planning and review;
- skills in applying their subject knowledge;
- skills in assessment, recording and reporting achievement;
- the ability to use and evaluate information technology (IT) across the curriculum.

(Adapted from: *The National Curriculum and the Initial Training of Student, Articled and Licensed Teachers*, NCC, April 1991.)

This book is a short introduction to the first three of these areas. It provides:

- an outline of the statutory framework;
- a summary of each National Curriculum subject Order and the requirements governing religious education (RE) in England and Wales;
- further sources of information and guidance about the National Curriculum available from the National Curriculum Council (NCC), the Curriculum Council for Wales (CCW), the Schools Examinations and Assessment Council (SEAC), Department for Education (DFE; formerly Department of Education and Science, DES), Welsh Office Education Department (WOED), and Her Majesty's Inspectorate (HMI);
- a guide to key National Curriculum terms, concepts and abbreviations.

The main audiences for the publication are student, articled and licensed teachers, particularly at the start of their initial training. It may also be useful to others who are 'new' to the National Curriculum, such as teachers returning to the profession after a career break.

The book has been produced jointly by NCC, CCW and SEAC.

PART ONE: THE STATUTORY FRAMEWORK

1. WHY A NATIONAL CURRICULUM?

Attendance at school in England and Wales has been compulsory by law since 1880. Yet, for more than a century, the law had nothing to say about what pupils were entitled to receive at school or what parents had a right to expect, apart from religious education. Over that period there were growing concerns about standards, the variable performance of schools, and inadequate information for parents and others.

Demand for a more clearly defined curriculum has grown strongly over the last few decades. A turning point was the speech at Ruskin College in 1976 by the then Prime Minister, Mr James Callaghan, in which he referred to 'the strong case for the so-called core curriculum of basic knowledge.'

Premature specialisation had deprived many pupils of a broad and balanced curriculum. For example, around three quarters of young people left school without attempting an examination covering a balanced science course. Sixty per cent or more did not study a modern foreign language beyond the age of 14. Moreover, there was a strong gender bias: very few girls took heavy craft subjects and few boys studied foreign languages.

These concerns culminated in the *Education Reform Act 1988* (ERA). ERA created the National Curriculum, which represents a turning point in the history of education in England and Wales. For the first time, a clear legal framework for raising standards in schools has been set.

2. AIMS OF THE NATIONAL CURRICULUM

The goal is for pupils to develop the knowledge, understanding and skills which they, and the country, will need in the twenty-first century.

Specifically, the National Curriculum aims to provide:

- clear and precise objectives for schools, based on best practice;
- identifiable targets for pupils to work towards;
- clear, accurate information for parents about what their children can be expected to know, understand and do, and what they actually achieve;
- guidance for teachers, to help them get the best possible results from each pupil;
- continuity and progression from one year to the next, and from one school to another.

3. KEY STAGES, AGES AND YEAR GROUPS

To emphasise the need for continuity from 5 to 16, ERA describes a pupil's progression through the years of compulsory education in **four key stages.** The stages will be the same whatever the local school organisation or transfer ages.

Table 1. Key stages, ages and year groups

Key Stage (KS)	Age of the majority of pupils at the end of the school year	New description of year groups
*	5	Reception (R)
KS1	6 7	Year 1 (Y1) Year 2 (Y2)
KS2	8 9 10 11	Year 3 (Y3) Year 4 (Y4) Year 5 (Y5) Year 6 (Y6)
KS3	12 13 14	Year 7 (Y7) Year 8 (Y8) Year 9 (Y9)
KS4	15 16	Year 10 (Y10) Year 11 (Y11)
**	17 18	Year 12 (Y12) Year 13 (Y13)

* Key Stage 1 (KS1) starts at the beginning of the term after a pupil's fifth birthday. It also includes those pupils in reception classes (R) who have reached compulsory school age. The description does not cover nursery provision.

** Years 12 and 13 are sometimes referred to as 'Key Stage 5' although this has no statutory basis; neither does the description of the year groups which has now been widely adopted by schools.

4. CORE AND FOUNDATION SUBJECTS

The National Curriculum is made up of **core** and other **foundation subjects** which are defined by law. At KS4 there is greater flexibility and choice for students. The requirements for KS1–3 and KS4 are set out in Tables 2 and 3, respectively.

Table 2. The National Curriculum for Key Stages 1–3

Core subjects	Subject	Abbreviation
	Mathematics	Ma
	Science	Sc
	English	En
	Welsh	We
Other foundation subjects	Welsh second language	WSL
	Technology	Te
	Modern foreign languages	MFL
	History	Hi
	Geography	Gg
	Art	Ar
	Music	Mu
	Physical education	PE

1. The codes shown in the shaded box are the accepted abbreviations for subject titles.
2. Technology includes design & technology (D&T) and information technology (IT).
3. A modern foreign language is not compulsory in KS1 and KS2.
4. Welsh is a core subject in schools in Wales where Welsh is the main medium of instruction. It is a foundation subject in schools in Wales where Welsh is not the main medium of instruction.
5. Technology and MFL are sometimes referred to, with the core subjects, as the **extended core.**

5. RELIGIOUS EDUCATION

Religious education is a compulsory element of the curriculum in England and Wales. Religious education and the National Curriculum are together referred to as **the Basic Curriculum**. Details are given on pages 56–57.

6. SCHOOLS AND THE NATIONAL CURRICULUM

The National Curriculum applies to all maintained schools including voluntary, special and grant-maintained schools, although the Secretaries of State may make specific exceptions where, for example, particular curriculum development projects are being undertaken. Independent schools do not have to follow the National Curriculum (although many do) and City Technology Colleges follow its main provisions as a condition of their grant.

The organisation of the school curriculum, within the statutory framework set by the *Education (No. 2) Act 1986* and ERA, is the responsibility of the headteacher.

Table 3. The National Curriculum for Key Stage 4

Core subjects	**National Curriculum requirement**
Mathematics	Full course
Science	Single science, double science or three separate sciences
English	Full course
Welsh	Full course
Other foundation subjects	
Welsh second language	Full or short course
Technology	Full course
A modern foreign language	Full or short course
History / Geography	Full course in one or short course in both
Physical education	Compulsory
Art	Optional
Music	Optional

1. A **short course** has less curriculum content and should require approximately half the teaching time of a full course.
2. Certification of National Curriculum subjects will be through the General Certificate of Secondary Education (GCSE) or equivalent. This is likely to apply to full courses, short courses and combined courses (e.g. a combination of two short courses).
3. Religious education continues to be compulsory at KS4.
4. Although art and music are not statutory, schools should offer some form of aesthetic experience in the curriculum for all 14–16 year olds. The great majority of schools should offer art and music to pupils who wish to continue their study of these subjects after 14.

It is for schools to decide:

- how much time should be spent on teaching the programme of study for a particular subject;
- how subjects are timetabled;
- the most appropriate teaching methods and materials to use.

7. PUPILS AND THE NATIONAL CURRICULUM

The National Curriculum is for all pupils in maintained schools. It is flexible enough to permit wide participation by pupils with special educational needs (SEN) without compromising its breadth and balance.

For **individual pupils** a statement of special educational needs under the *Education Act 1981* may specify disapplication or modification of particular aspects of the National Curriculum. There is, however, considerable flexibility for pupils at either end of the ability range to work within the National Curriculum, e.g. individual pupils can study material which is outside the normal range expected for pupils of their age. Pupils within a key stage or class may well be working at different levels at the same time .

For **groups of pupils** there is also considerable flexibility, e.g. whole classes of very able pupils may complete their National Curriculum studies early in one or more subjects, before the end of KS4.

In order to enable **pupils with special educational needs but no statements** to have access to the National Curriculum, it is for schools, in consultation with parents and the local education authority (LEA), to decide:

- which pupils have special educational needs;
- whether the flexibility allowed for in the National Curriculum helps these pupils to progress;
- whether modifications to the National Curriculum requirements are needed and a statement of special educational need should be drawn up.

In order to enable **pupils with statements of special educational needs** to have access to the National Curriculum, it is for schools, in consultation with the parents and the LEA, to decide:

- which programmes of study can be taught to individual pupils, so that they are offered a broad and balanced curriculum in line with their individual needs;
- what other curricular priorities should be specified in the statement in order to meet the pupil's special educational needs;
- whether National Curriculum end of key stage assessment is the best way of indicating their pupils' progress and how that progress should be reported.

In all cases the main criterion for deciding whether to exercise this sort of flexibility should be the best educational interests of the individual pupil.

8. PARENTS AND THE NATIONAL CURRICULUM

Parents need to be kept informed about what their children will be learning at school and how they are progressing.

Published in October 1991, the *Parent's Charter* listed five key documents which parents have a right to receive:

- an annual report on the child;
- regular reports from independent inspectors;
- performance tables for all local schools;
- a prospectus or brochure about the school;
- an annual governors' report on the school.

THE ANNUAL REPORT

The charter proposed that the annual report should include:

- comments on the pupil's progress in National Curriculum subjects;
- the pupil's level of attainment in each subject at the end of each key stage following statutory assessment at ages 7, 11, 14 and 16;
- results of other examinations or tests taken during the year;
- comments on the pupil's achievements in other subjects beside those of the National Curriculum and in other activities;
- comparison between the individual's results in examinations and national tests with those of others in the same group, and the national average;
- a comment from the headteacher or class teacher on general progress and attendance record;
- an indication of the person to whom the parent should talk to discuss the report, and details of how to fix an appointment.

(Taken from the *Parent's Charter,* DES October 1991.)

9. THE NATIONAL CURRICULUM TIMETABLE

ERA required the Secretaries of State to establish the National Curriculum 'as soon as is reasonably practicable', with advice from advisory bodies and consultation procedures provided for in the Act. By the autumn of 1992, all the National Curriculum Orders will be in place. Table 4 shows how National Curriculum requirements progressively apply to pupils in each year group.

Each subject of the National Curriculum is defined in a separate Order, which the Secretaries of State must lay before Parliament for approval. These are provided in separate ringbinders. ERA provides for the Secretaries of State to make amendments to the Orders in the light of advice received from the Curriculum and Assessment Councils (see Section 10). This has already happened in the case of mathematics and science. The 1989 Orders were simplified in 1991 to make planning, assessment and recording more manageable for teachers. The content of the mathematics and science curriculum remained virtually unchanged. In June 1992 the Secretaries of State also announced a review of the technology Order (see page 36), and in September 1992, a review of the English Order (see page 31).

10. THE CURRICULUM AND ASSESSMENT COUNCILS

NCC, CCW and SEAC were established under ERA in August 1988.

The general functions of **NCC** and **CCW** are:

- to keep all aspects of the curriculum for maintained schools under review;
- to advise the Secretaries of State on the curriculum for maintained schools;
- to carry out programmes of research and development connected with the school curriculum;
- to publish and disseminate information relating to the curriculum.

Table 4. Timetable for the introduction of National Curriculum subjects*

KS	1		2				3			4	
Year	1	2	3	4	5	6	7	8	9	10	11
Ma	89	90	90	91	92	93	89	90	91	92	93
Sc	89	90	90	91	92	93	89	90	91	92	93
En	89	90	90	91	92	93	90	91	92	92	93
We**	90	91	90	91	92	93	90	91	92	93	94
WSL***	92	93	94	95	96	97	92	93	94	95	96
Te	90	91	90	91	92	93	90	91	92	93	94
Hi	91	92	91	92	93	94	91	92	93	94	95
Gg	91	92	91	92	93	94	91	92	93	94	95
MFL							92	93	94	95	96
Ar	92	93	92	93	94	95	92	93	94	95	96
Mu	92	93	92	93	94	95	92	93	94	95	96
PE	92	93	92	93	94	95	92	93	94	95	96

* Subjects are introduced in the autumn term.
** Pupils in schools where Welsh is currently taught.
*** Pupils in other schools in Wales.

NCC's and CCW's responsibilities include all aspects of the school curriculum, not just the foundation subjects, as well as the curriculum for under fives and for 16–19 year olds. The Councils' remits take account of ethnic and cultural diversity and the need for the curriculum to provide equal opportunities for all pupils, including pupils with special educational needs.

The general functions of **SEAC** are:

- to keep all aspects of examinations and assessment under review;
- to advise the Secretaries of State on examinations and assessment;
- to advise on, and if requested carry out, programmes of research and development connected with examinations and assessment;
- to publish and disseminate information relating to examinations and assessment;
- to make arrangements with appropriate bodies for the moderation of assessments as part of the assessment arrangements;
- to advise the Secretaries of State on the exercise of their powers under Section 5(1) of ERA (relating to the statutory approval of qualifications and syllabuses for pupils 5–16).

All three Councils may also be asked to undertake specific additional duties or tasks by the Secretaries of State.

(Adapted from ERA, Section 14)

In the White Paper, *Choice and Diversity: A New Framework for Schools*, published on 28 July 1992, the Government set out its proposals for the establishment of a new **School Curriculum and Assessment Authority** (SCAA) with responsibility in England for ensuring quality in the curriculum and the associated assessment arrangements. The new body is likely to take over the present roles and functions of NCC and SEAC in 1993 or early 1994. In Wales, the Government proposes to extend the functions of CCW to include responsibility for the assessment of Welsh at KS1–4 and beyond and the assessment of all other subjects at KS1–3. The proposed new body will be called the **Curriculum and Assessment Authority for Wales** (CAAW).

11. NATIONAL CURRICULUM ASSESSMENT, RECORDING AND REPORTING

Assessment is a central feature of the National Curriculum. At, or near the end of, each key stage teachers are required to summarise their pupils' achievements. In most subjects this will be in the form of a level in each attainment target (see Part Two) on the basis of both continuous 'teacher assessment' done throughout the key stage, and nationally set tasks or tests carried out at the end of the key stage*.

TEACHER ASSESSMENT

The main purpose of teacher assessment is to build up a picture of pupils' achievements over each key stage in relation to the National Curriculum, in order to take pupils forward in their learning. This information is then summarised at the end of each key stage.

---

* For art, music and physical education at the end of KS1–3, teachers will assess pupils' attainments against more general end of key stage statements. There will be no standard national tests or tasks.

Teacher assessment is part of everyday teaching and learning. It is a continuous process, not a separate activity which necessarily requires the use of extra tasks or tests. The National Curriculum provides a framework for identifying pupils' attainments in the form of a national structure of assessment objectives which will help teachers recognise pupils' achievements and ensure progress and continuity in learning.

Some key features of teacher assessment are outlined below.

Using professional judgement

Teachers must make their own judgements about their pupils' achievements in relation to attainment targets, statements of attainment and end of key stage statements. The point at which a teacher is satisfied that a statement has been achieved will vary from pupil to pupil and with different statements. Discussions with other teachers about how and why judgements have been made are important in trying to achieve consistent interpretations of statements of attainment and end of key stage statements. SEAC's *Children's/Pupils' Work Assessed* series of publications shows examples of pupils' work along with judgements that have been made in relation to statements of attainment and attainment targets. This material, together with the national tasks and tests, should help these discussions.

Involving pupils in their own assessment

Teacher assessment can help pupils to understand what they are learning and to chart their own progress. Pupils can be actively involved in their own assessment: reviewing their work and progress; setting future targets for learning; and deciding,in discussion with teachers, which pieces of work provide evidence of particular attainments.

Recording attainment

Attainment should be recorded throughout the key stage. These records can help in planning future work. They can form a basis for identifying pupils' achievements in relation to the attainment targets, statements of attainment and end of key stage statements. The purposes of any recording arrangements should be clear to all who work with them. Recording should not be unwieldy or time consuming or get in the way of teaching and learning. How records are kept should be regularly reviewed to ensure they remain manageable.

Collecting evidence

Evidence of pupils' attainment comes in many forms, not all of which are written. Evidence gained through observation should also be taken into account when judgements are made and recorded. It is important to be able to point to examples of achievement which support particular judgements. It is not, however, necessary to collect evidence of everything a pupil does. Collections of pupils' work with teachers' notes can be particularly useful when pupils transfer between schools during or at the end of a key stage.

Reporting to parents

Section 8 of this book sets out some issues related to parents and the National Curriculum. Knowledge about pupils' achievements built up through Teacher Assessment can help to make reports as useful as possible. Parents will need help to become familiar with the National Curriculum framework so that they can more easily understand how their children are progressing. Continuous teacher assessment can also help to involve parents in their children's learning.

END OF KEY STAGE ASSESSMENT

Table 5 shows the timetable for the introduction of National Curriculum assessment for each key stage.

Key Stages 1–3

In most subjects at the end of KS1, KS2 and KS3, teachers are required to summarise their own assessments in the form of a level for each attainment target. In addition they are required to set their pupils nationally prescribed tasks or tests*. At KS1 and KS2, the use of the tasks in subjects other than mathematics, science, English and Welsh is voluntary. These and other tasks at KS1 and KS2 should help to inform Teacher Assessment.

Table 5. Timetable for National Curriculum Assessment

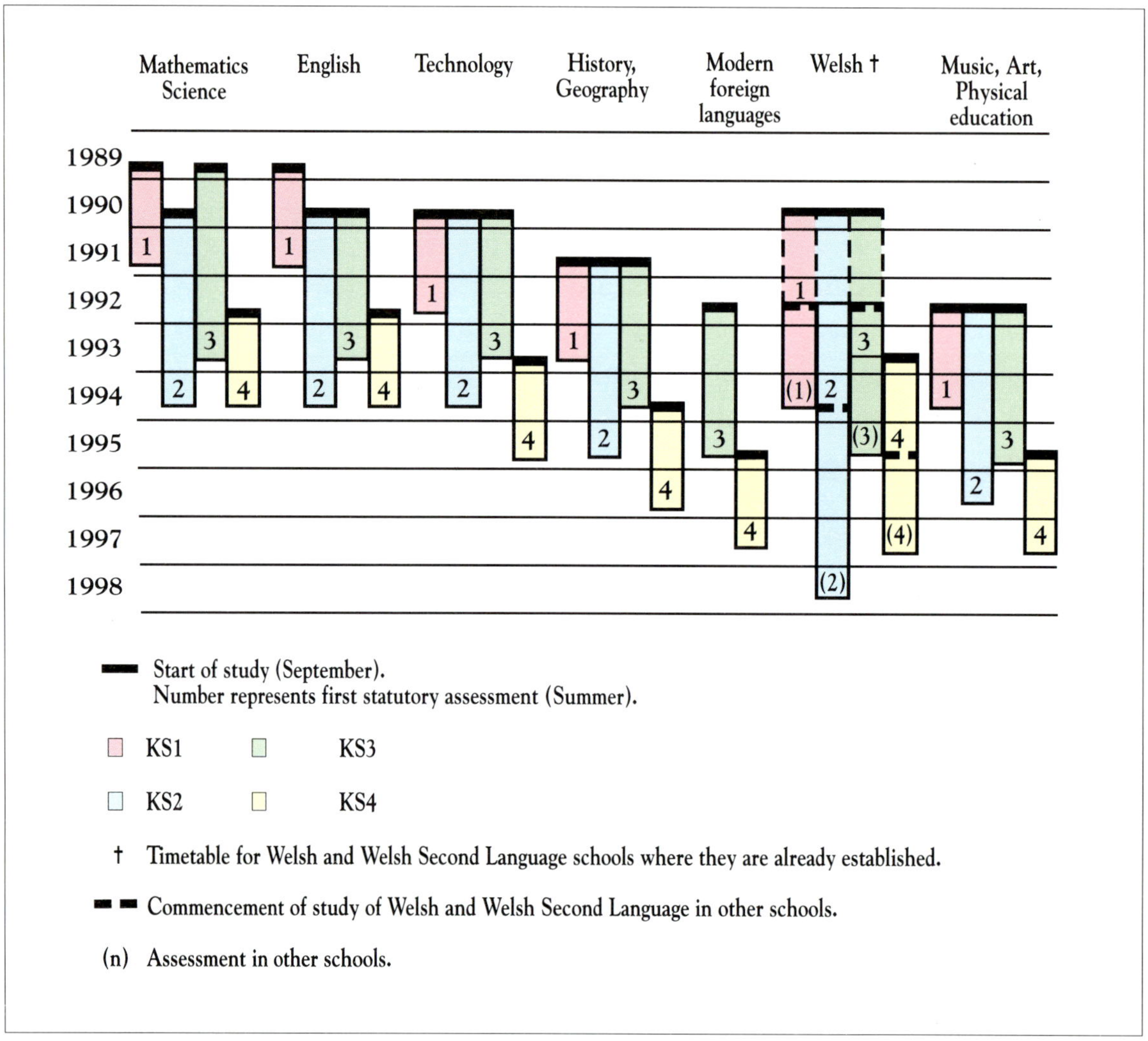

The purposes of the statutory end of key stage tasks and tests are to:

- provide a 'snapshot' of pupils' attainment at the key ages of 7, 11 and 14, for pupils, teachers and parents to inform the next stage of education;
- show teachers and the public how successful schools have been in relation to a national standard;
- enable standards nationally to be compared from one year to the next.

* See earlier note about art, music and physical education where the requirements are different.

Precise end of key stage arrangements differ between subjects and key stages. Table 6 summarises the current position. SEAC produces *School Assessment Folders* which contain up-to-date information for teachers about end of key stage procedures.

Key Stage 4

The main form of assessment at the end of KS4 is GCSE or equivalent examinations. New subject criteria and syllabuses are being introduced in accordance with the National Curriculum timetable. New coursework limits also apply to National Curriculum subjects, as shown in Table 7. The GCSE will cover National Curriculum Levels 4–10. From 1994 results from GCSE will be given in the form of these levels for all subjects. Separate assessment arrangements will apply for those pupils whose attainment is below Level 4. Table 8 shows how the levels match up with the previous letter grades.

Table 6. National tasks/tests and teacher assessment at Key Stages 1–3

	KS1		KS2		KS3	
Subject	**National tasks/tests**	**Teacher assessment**	**National tasks/tests**	**Teacher assessment**	**National tasks/tests**	**Teacher assessment**
Ma	✔	✔	✔	✔	✔	✔
Sc	✔	✔	✔	✔	✔	✔
En	✔	✔	✔	✔	✔	✔
We	✔	✔	✔	✔	✔	✔
WSL	*	✔	*	✔	✔	✔
Te	*	✔	*	✔	✔	✔
Hi	*	✔	*	✔	✔	✔
Gg	*	✔	*	✔	✔	✔
MFL	N/A		N/A		✔	✔
Ar	–	✔	–	✔	–	✔
Mu	–	✔	–	✔	–	✔
PE	–	✔	–	✔	–	✔

* Non-mandatory tests will be available in these subjects at KS1 and KS2 for teachers to administer as and when they cover the programmes of study and, in the process, to build up a record of pupil knowledge, understanding and skill in these subjects.

Table 7. Coursework limits for Key Stage 4

Course beginning	Subject	Coursework limits
September 1992	Mathematics	20%
	Science	30%
	English	40% *
September 1993	Biology	30%
	Chemistry	30%
	Physics	30%
	Welsh	40% **
	Welsh Second Language	40%
	Technology	60%
September 1994	History	25%
	Geography	25%
September 1995	Modern Foreign Languages (provisional)	30%

* Up to 20% for Attainment Target 1 (Speaking and Listening) and up to 20% between Attainment Targets 2 and 3 (Reading and Writing).

** Not less than 20% for Attainment Target 1 (Oral) and between 10% and 20% for Attainment Targets 2 and 3 (Reading and Writing).

Table 8. GCSE Scale of Awards

The GCSE scale of awards up to and including 1993	The GCSE scale of awards from 1994 onwards
	10
A	9
B	8
C	
	7
D	
	6
E	
F	5
G	4

12. CROSS-CURRICULAR ELEMENTS

Section 1 of ERA places a responsibility on schools to provide a broad and balanced curriculum which:

a) *promotes the spiritual, moral, cultural, mental and physical development of pupils at the school and of society; and*

b) *prepares such pupils for the opportunities, responsibilities and experiences of adult life.*

NCC's and CCW's view of the whole curriculum and ways of describing it are slightly different.

NCC'S VIEW OF THE WHOLE CURRICULUM (DIMENSIONS, SKILLS AND THEMES)

NCC's publication *Curriculum Guidance 3: The Whole Curriculum* (1990), identifies three cross-curricular elements which have a key role to play in helping schools to provide a curriculum which fulfils the above requirements. These elements are:

- dimensions;
- skills;
- themes.

For all pupils, but particularly pupils with special educational needs, curriculum breadth and balance will be enhanced through work on cross-curricular skills and themes. Together with the dimensions these elements should be an explicit part of the curriculum policy in every school and integral to the planning, development and evaluation of a school's curriculum.

Dimensions

The dimensions cover all aspects of equal opportunities and education for life in a multicultural society.

Providing equal opportunities for all pupils means:

- treating pupils as individuals with their own abilities, difficulties, attitudes, backgrounds and experiences;
- challenging myths, stereotypes and misconceptions;
- ensuring that equal access to the curriculum means real opportunity to benefit.

Educating pupils for life in a multicultural society means:

- extending pupils' knowledge and understanding of different cultures, languages and faiths;
- valuing cultural diversity by drawing on pupils' backgrounds and experiences;
- offering positive images and role models from all cultures.

The dimensions permeate the curriculum and are the responsibility of all teachers.

Skills

Skills can be developed coherently throughout the curriculum provided that teachers adhere to the principle of sharing responsibility. NCC has identified six cross-curricular skills which can be developed through National Curriculum subjects and religious education. These skills are:

- communication;
- numeracy;
- study;
- problem solving;
- personal and social;
- information technology.

Themes

NCC has named five themes which it considers to be particularly important in helping to prepare pupils to take an active and informed part in adult life.

- **Economic and industrial understanding** (EIU) covers: financial decision-making; economic roles (e.g. producers, consumers and citizens); government economic policy; and the impact of economic activity on the environment.
- **Careers education and guidance** covers five areas: self, roles, career, transition, work.
- **Health education** covers: use and misuse of various substances, sex education, family life education, safety, nutrition, personal hygiene, health-related exercise, environmental and psychological aspects.
- **Education for citizenship** covers: participative citizenship; information on which to base the development of skills, values and attitudes towards citizenship; local, regional, national and international community relationships including the European dimension; democracy; human rights; law; employment; public services and leisure.
- **Environmental education** covers: responsible attitudes towards the environment; knowledge and understanding of the processes by which environments are shaped; the vulnerability of different environments; and opportunities for protecting and managing the environment.

The themes can be related to all National Curriculum subjects and religious education.In some cases they act as contexts for the development of subject-specific skills, in others they are part of the prescribed content of a particular subject. The examples below indicate how subjects and the themes might relate. This is not an exhaustive list.

Mathematics

The themes provide a context in which many aspects of the programmes of study may be taught, for example:

- using and applying mathematics in a mini-enterprise scheme;
- interpreting data related to an environmental or health issue.

Science

The programmes of study for science require exploration of how science is applied in a variety of contexts, including society, industry and the environment. These contexts fall within the scope of the five themes. Economic and industrial understanding, health education and environmental education are of particular relevance.

English

The themes provide many opportunities for work in all the attainment targets in English. They offer a source of issues and a purposeful context for the development of skills and understanding. For example, an issue from Environmental Education might provide the focus for a drama-based project and the development of higher order reading skills for the retrieval of information from non-fiction sources.

Technology

Contexts stipulated for the study of technology include home, community, recreation, business and industry. The themes fit naturally into studies based on these contexts.

History

A general requirement of the programme of study for history is that pupils should have opportunities in each key stage to 'develop knowledge, understanding and skills related to cross-curricular themes, in particular citizenship, environmental, health and careers education, and education for economic and industrial understanding.'

Geography
Environmental education, economic and industrial understanding, careers education and citizenship all feature in the requirements for geography.

Modern foreign languages
The content and contexts for developing language skills are set out as seven 'areas of experience' which embrace the five themes. For example, Area C (The World Around Us) has clear links with environmental education. Area D (The World of Education, Training and Work) is of direct relevance to careers education and guidance.

Art
The themes can provide a focus for art activities, e.g. environmental education can be used as a stimulus for the deployment of skills such as perception and planning.

Music
The themes can provide a focus for activities and a stimulus for creative work. Music can also provide a context for the teaching of cross-curricular themes.

Physical education
The most relevant theme in physical education is health education, particularly the health-related exercise component. The other themes gain increasing relevance in KS4, especially where an examination course is being pursued.

Religious education
All the themes feature in religious education. For example, concern for the environment often has a religious rationale, as does the development of personal responsibility and human rights along with other dimensions of citizenship. Religious teachings often lie at the foundation of attitudes to sex-education, an aspect of health education.

CCW'S VIEW OF THE WHOLE CURRICULUM (ASPECTS OF LEARNING, THEMES, COMPETENCES, DIMENSIONS)

CCW's publication *The Whole Curriculum 5–16 in Wales* (1991) identifies in a similar way matters which schools will need to consider in their planning. These are:

- aspects of learning which together describe the whole curriculum; and
- themes, competences and dimensions which, when taken with the statutory and other subjects, give the curriculum coherence and relevance.

Aspects of learning
In planning broad and balanced provision for pupils, CCW suggests that schools should consider the curriculum as comprising eight inherently cross-curricular aspects of learning which together describe the full range of experiences to which pupils are entitled. These aspects are the:

- expressive and aesthetic;
- linguistic and literary;
- mathematical;
- physical and recreational;
- scientific;
- social and environmental;
- spiritual and moral;
- technological.

Properly developed, these aspects of learning should enable the curriculum to be planned and developed as a whole, enabling schools to consider the contributions made by the National Curriculum and other subjects and the links and relationships between them.

This process will emphasise the essential wholeness of the curriculum and the ways in which its different elements interact. The fact that 'subjects' do not equate with aspects of learning cannot be over-emphasised.

Themes, competences and dimensions

National Curriculum subjects and religious education are vitally important (and statutory) elements of the aspects of learning which make up the curriculum. Schools will also need to consider how their provision for pupils reflects the basic requirements of ERA. If pupils are to experience a curriculum which genuinely promotes their personal and social development careful planning for particular themes, competences and dimensions which go across curricular boundaries will be needed.

Themes

Access to certain elements of learning will help pupils to take an active and informed part in the world at large.

- **Careers education and guidance** which, as with NCC, covers five areas: self; roles; career; transition; work.
- **Community understanding** is a theme distinctive to Wales intended to meet the needs of young people growing up in Wales. It is concerned with helping pupils identify and appreciate the common experience of their cultural heritage as well as understand its diverse and distinctive aspects. It encourages them to contribute, as active, participating, critically reflective members of their communities in Wales, or wherever they may subsequently live. Pupils should be encouraged to explore relevant contexts such as: becoming a member of a community; patterns of social life; active citizenship; human rights; participation in decision making; order, conflict and change; people, work and the distribution of resources; values and beliefs.
- **Economic and industrial understanding** is concerned with providing pupils with opportunities to acquire: a knowledge and critical understanding of the nature, causes and effects of economic activity; relative analytical, personal and social skills; those attitudes which will allow them to play a full and responsible part in economic and industrial decision making. Pupils should be encouraged to explore relevant contexts such as consumer affairs; industry, business and the world of work; the Welsh, UK, European and world economies; and environmental and community issues such as industrial pollution, unemployment and poverty.
- **Environmental education** aims to provide structured opportunities for young people to investigate issues of environmental concern, while at the same time acquiring an informed and critical understanding of the effects of actions and decisions taken now on the future of the environment.
- **Health education:** current thinking sees a concern for health knowledge and understanding, the fostering of positive attitudes to health and the development of skills for a healthy lifestyle permeating the curriculum as a whole. Pupils should be encouraged to explore relevant contexts such as: substance use and misuse; sex

education; family life education; safety; health-related exercise; food and nutrition; personal hygiene; environmental aspects of health education; psychological aspects of health education.

Although associated with particular knowledge, understanding and competences, much of the content of the themes is already present within the programmes of study of the National Curriculum subjects. However, schools need to ensure that teachers identify the opportunities, within their subjects, to develop the themes. Primary school provision will often be made within 'thematic' or topic-based work. Secondary schools should integrate themes within teaching programmes for particular subjects supplemented where necessary by specific additional activities or through personal and social education courses.

Competences

Different aspects of learning will provide a range of contexts and opportunities through which a number of key competences can be delivered and fostered. It is very important that schools should agree on coherent, cross-curricular approaches to the development of pupils' capabilities in relation to:

- communication (including literacy and oracy);
- the use of information technology;
- numeracy;
- problem solving;
- studying.

Dimensions

In planning provision, schools will need to consider positively the way in which dimensions should underpin the curriculum, and permeate the planning of the whole curriculum. Such dimensions play a vital role in developing a pupil's attitudes and understanding and include:

- the fostering of sympathetic awareness and understanding of the cultural diversity of society;
- provision of equal opportunities for all pupils, irrespective of gender, ability or cultural and ethnic background;
- catering for the special needs of pupils in ways which make the curriculum accessible to all pupils;
- demonstration of the cultural relevance of the curriculum to its Welsh setting.

PART TWO: THE NATIONAL CURRICULUM STATUTORY ORDERS AND RELIGIOUS EDUCATION

1. FROM WORKING GROUP TO STATUTORY ORDER

Each National Curriculum subject has gone through a number of stages, including:

- the appointment of a working group by the Secretaries of State to advise on attainment targets and programmes of study for that subject;
- publication of each working group's reports (an interim and final report*);
- formal proposals by the Secretaries of State based on the working group's recommendations;
- statutory consultation on these proposals carried out in England by NCC, and in Wales by WOED on behalf of the Secretary of State for Wales;
- in England advice from NCC to the Secretary of State, in Wales the Secretary of State for Wales is statutorily obliged to consult CCW;
- publication of a draft Order (with formal consultation conducted by the DES** and WOED);
- publication of the final Order setting out attainment targets, programmes of study and dates of implementation. Copies, in ring binders, are sent to schools in England by the DFE and to schools in Wales by the Welsh Office.

Table 9 sets out the timetable for each National Curriculum subject. Religious education does not have nationally prescribed attainment targets or programmes of study (see page 56).

2. ATTAINMENT TARGETS AND PROGRAMMES OF STUDY

The following definitions explain the meaning of attainment targets, programmes of study and other associated terms. (The appendix contains a glossary of National Curriculum key terms, concepts and abbreviations.)

ATTAINMENT TARGETS (ATs)

Objectives for each foundation subject setting out the knowledge, skills and understanding which pupils of different abilities and maturities are expected to develop in each subject.
For example:

English AT1:	Speaking and listening
Geography AT2:	Knowledge and understanding of places

---

* The final report of each working group is a useful source of reference. It explains the rationale and thinking which underpins the attainment targets and programmes of study . It is published with the proposals of the Secretaries of State. Dates of publication are shown in Table 9.

** The DES officially changed its name to the DFE (Department for Education) on 6 July 1992.

Table 9. From working group to implementation

Subject	Working group set up	Proposals of Secretaries of State published	Implementation: autumn term
Mathematics	July 1987	August 1988	1989
Science	July 1987	August 1988	1989
English	April 1988 (5–7) (5–16)	November 1988 June 1989	1989 1990
Welsh	April 1988	October 1988	1990
Welsh second language	April 1988	October 1988	1990* 1992**
Technology	April 1988	June 1989	1990
History	January 1989	July 1990	1991
Geography	May 1989	June 1990	1991
Modern foreign languages	August 1989	October 1990	1992
Art	July 1990	August 1991	1992
Music	July 1990	August 1991	1992
Physical education	July 1990	August 1991	1992

1. The English working group was able to report first on KS1 and KS2. The statutory Order for KS1 was published in May 1989.
2. The dates for implementation shown in this table apply only to the first year of relevant key stages. Table 4 gives fuller details of the timetable for the introduction of each subject.

* Applies to schools where Welsh is taught.

** Applies to other schools in Wales.

PROGRAMMES OF STUDY (PoS)

The matters, skills and processes which must be taught to pupils during each key stage in order to meet the objectives set out in the ATs.

The nature and structure of PoS and ATs, and the relationship between them, vary from subject to subject.

For example:

Mathematics has a PoS for each AT which is level related (i.e. the PoS specifies material to be taught to pupils working within particular levels of attainment).

English has PoS which are key stage related (i.e. the PoS set out what pupils should experience during each key stage).

In **history,** the PoS include specific 'study units' for each key stage.

In **modern foreign languages** the PoS include broad areas of content as well as the skills to be developed in learning and using the target language.

STRANDS

The term 'strand' is used to describe a sequence of related SoA or ideas running through an AT or PoS. In most subjects it is possible to identify certain key ideas or aspects which can be traced through several levels of an AT and from one key stage to the next. Strands are more explicit and more systematically developed in some subjects (e.g. mathematics and science) than in others (e.g. English).

For example:

Science identifies strands in each AT which describe the development of pupils' scientific ideas. For example, in AT3 'chemical changes' is one of the strands relating to materials and their properties.

Technology AT5 has five main strands which relate to different aspects of the development of pupils' information technology capability.

LEVELS OF ATTAINMENT

These are the different levels defined within each AT, reflecting differences in ability and progress. In most subjects each AT has 10 levels covering all four key stages. Figure 1 shows the 10-level scale based on the model in the TGAT Report (Task Group on Assessment and Testing, December 1987). Table 10 sets out the range of levels within which most pupils will be working in different subjects at each key stage.

STATEMENTS OF ATTAINMENT (SoA)

Each level of attainment in an AT is defined by more precise objectives called SoA.

For example:

Level 1 of **modern foreign languages** AT1 (Listening) has two SoA. Pupils should be able to:

a) understand and respond to familiar utterances of up to four words;

b) identify individual items in a list.

END OF KEY STAGE STATEMENTS (EKSS)

For art, music and physical education, where the 10-level scale and SoA do not operate, there are more general end of key stage statements (EKSS). These are statutory statements representing the knowledge, skills and understanding which pupils of different abilities and maturities can be expected to achieve by the end of the key stage in question.

For example:

Music – by the end of KS1 pupils should be able to 'talk in simple but appropriate terms about sounds they have made, listened to, performed or composed' (AT2).

Figure 1. The TGAT model

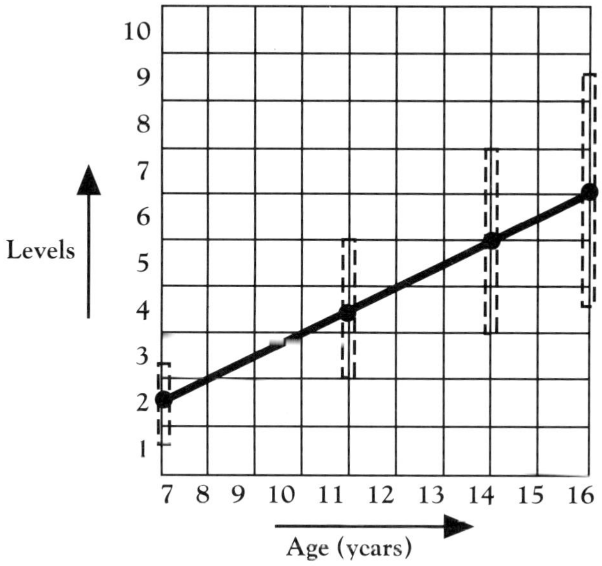

1. The bold line shows the average levels expected of pupils at the ages specified.
2. The dotted lines represent the possible range within which the great majority of pupils might demonstrate attainment.

Table 10. Levels by key stages

Subject	**KS1 5–7 years**	**KS2 7–11 years**	**KS3 11–14 years**	**KS4 14–16 years**
Mathematics	1–3	2–6	3–8	4–10
Science	1–3	2–5	3–7	4–10
English	1–3	2–5	3–8	3–10
Welsh	1–3	2–5	3–8	3–10
Welsh second language	1–3	2–5	3–8/1–6*	3–10
Technology	1–3	2–5	3–7	4–10
Modern foreign languages	–	–	1–10	1–10
History	1–3	2–5	3–7	4–10
Geography	1–3	2–5	3–7	4–10
Art Music Physical education	} Not applicable			

1. Shading indicates key differences between subjects.
2. It is expected that the attainment of the great majority of pupils at the end of each key stage will fall within the ranges of level specified above. The attainment of most pupils is likely to lie at or close to the middle of these ranges.
3. There is considerable flexibility for teachers to use material from PoS and to address SoA at levels outside those specified for a particular key stage (e.g. with higher of lower achieving pupils).

* For those beginning Welsh second language at 11.

3. SUMMARIES OF NATIONAL CURRICULUM SUBJECT ORDERS AND RELIGIOUS EDUCATION

The summaries which follow set out for each National Curriculum subject essential information about:

- ATs;
- strands;
- PoS;
- key stages and levels;
- the timetable for implementation;
- the Order for Wales (where this differs from the Order for England).

Some summaries end with a **special note** highlighting particular issues relevant to that subject but not to others.

Full details of all subjects are contained in the statutory Orders and non-statutory guidance (NSG) produced by NCC and CCW.

The final section summarises the legal position of religious education as part of the basic curriculum in England and Wales. It provides general guidance only and should not be seen as comprehensive.

MATHEMATICS

ATTAINMENT TARGETS

ATs		Strands	
AT1	**Using and applying mathematics**	(i)	Applications
		(ii)	Mathematical communication
		(iii)	Reasoning, logic and proof
AT2	**Number**	(i)	Knowledge and use of numbers
		(ii)	Estimation and approximation
		(iii)	Measures
AT3	**Algebra**	(i)	Patterns and relationships
		(ii)	Formulae, equations and inequalities
		(iii)	Graphical representation
AT4	**Shape and space**	(i)	Shape
		(ii)	Location
		(iii)	Movement
		(iv)	Measures
AT5	**Handling data**	(i)	Collecting and processing
		(ii)	Representing and interpreting
		(iii)	Probability

STRANDS

SoA can be set out in strands that describe how important mathematical ideas develop through the National Curriculum levels. These are shown above in relation to each AT.

PROGRAMMES OF STUDY

There is a PoS for each AT. Each PoS consists of elements which correspond to each of the 10 levels of attainment.

The layout of the revised Order shows PoS, SoA and examples alongside each other. The elements of the PoS are necessary in determining the scope of each SoA and should be used to plan work for pupils in order for them to achieve the assessment objectives.

The PoS for AT1 needs to be considered in conjunction with the PoS for ATs 2-5:

- work related to ATs 2-5 provides the basis of knowledge and skills necessary for pupils to use and apply mathematics in the range of ways indicated in AT1;

- work related to AT1 provides the contexts and strategies through which pupils can extend the skills and understanding dealt with in ATs 2-5.

KEY STAGES/LEVELS

KS1	Levels 1–3
KS2	Levels 2–6
KS3	Levels 3–8
KS4	Levels 4–10

TIMETABLE

	KS1	**KS2**	**KS3**	**KS4**
ATs and PoS first apply (August)	1989	1990	1989	1992
Statutory assessment (Summer)	1991	1994	1993	1994

THE ORDER FOR WALES

The Order for Wales is the same as for England.

SPECIAL NOTE

The initial Order for mathematics was made in 1989. In January 1991 the Secretary of State announced a review of the attainment target structure. Following statutory consultations a new mathematics Order was laid before Parliament in December 1991. This came into force on 1 August 1992 and superseded the 1989 Order. The current Order has fewer ATs but the content of the mathematics curriculum remains substantially unchanged.

SCIENCE

ATTAINMENT TARGETS

ATs			Strands
AT1	**Scientific investigation**	(i)	Ask questions, predict and hypothesise
		(ii)	Observe, measure and manipulate variables
		(iii)	Interpret their results and evaluate scientific evidence
AT2	**Life and living processes**	(i)	Life processes and the organisation of living things
		(ii)	Variation and the mechanisms of inheritance and evolution
		(iii)	Populations and human influences within ecosystems
		(iv)	Energy flows and cycles of matter within ecosystems
AT3	**Materials and their properties**	(i)	The properties, classification and structure of materials
		(ii)	Explanations of the properties of materials
		(iii)	Chemical changes
		(iv)	The Earth and its atmosphere
AT4	**Physical processes**	(i)	Electricity and magnetism
		(ii)	Energy resources and energy transfer
		(ii)	Forces and their effects
		(iv)	Light and sound
		(v)	The Earth's place in the Universe

STRANDS

Each AT is composed of strands that describe how the main scientific ideas develop through National Curriculum levels. These are shown above in relation to each AT.

PROGRAMMES OF STUDY

There is a PoS for each AT in each key stage. In the Order, the PoS are displayed on the same pages as the SoA for a particular AT. The PoS are helpful in determining the scope of each AT.

The PoS for ATs 2–4 cover knowledge and understanding. The PoS for AT1 describes the skills of scientific investigation which allow pupils to explore the contexts provided in ATs 2–4. AT1 should be taught in relation to the PoS for other ATs.

KEY STAGES/LEVELS

KS1	Levels 1–3
KS2	Levels 2–5
KS3	Levels 3–7
KS4	Levels 4–10

TIMETABLE

	KS1	**KS2**	**KS3**	**KS4**
ATs and PoS first apply (August)	1989	1990	1989	1992
First statutory assessment (Summer)	1991	1994	1993	1994

THE ORDER FOR WALES

The Order for Wales is the same as for England.

SPECIAL NOTES

1. The majority of pupils in KS4 will follow a course of study covering all the ATs and all the strands. This will, for most pupils, lead to a **double** GCSE in science. Some pupils may wish to study a reduced course — **single** science, leading to a single GCSE. Pupils may also study three separate science GCSEs.
2. The initial Order for science was made in 1989. In January 1991 the Secretary of State announced a review of the AT structure. Following statutory consultations a new science Order was laid before Parliament in December 1991. This came into force on 1 August 1992 and superseded the 1989 Order. The current Order has fewer ATs but the content of the science curriculum remains substantially unchanged.

ATTAINMENT TARGETS

AT1	**Speaking and listening**	The development of pupils' understanding of the spoken word and the capacity to express themselves effectively in a variety of speaking and listening activities, matching style and response to audience and purpose.
AT2	**Reading**	The development of the ability to read, understand and respond to all types of writing, as well as the development of information-retrieval strategies for the purposes of study.
AT3	**Writing**	A growing ability to construct and convey meaning in written language, matching style to audience and purpose.
AT4	**Spelling**	Levels 1–4
AT5	**Handwriting**	
AT4/5	**Presentation**	Levels 5–7

STRANDS

It is possible to identify a number of strands in the English ATs and SoA, though these are not systematically developed over all 10 levels. For example, there is a strand relating to **knowledge about language** which starts at Level 5 in all ATs. Other strands are specific to each AT, e.g. group discussion (AT1), drafting (AT3), information-retrieval skills (AT2).

PROGRAMMES OF STUDY

Three PoS are defined:

1. Speaking and listening

a) for Key Stage 1
b) for Key Stages 2 to 4

These cover the range of situations, audiences and activities designed to develop pupils' competence, precision and confidence in speaking and listening.

2. Reading

a) for Key Stage 1
b) for Key Stage 2
c) for Key Stages 3 and 4

These cover the range of reading material and the knowledge, skills and understanding to be developed.

3. **Writing, Spelling and Handwriting**
   a) for Key Stage 1
   b) for Key Stage 2
   c) for Key Stages 3 and 4

These cover the range of contexts, purposes and audiences for writing; the conventions of writing and the knowledge about written language to be developed.

PoS are key stage related. Each PoS contains **general provisions** for the PoS as a whole and **detailed provisions** for the key stage or key stages which it covers. For most ATs these detailed provisions include material specifying what pupils working towards a particular level should experience.

KEY STAGES/LEVELS

KS1	Levels 1–3
KS2	Levels 2–5
KS3	Levels 3–8
KS4	Levels 3–10

TIMETABLE

	KS1	**KS2**	**KS3**	**KS4**
ATs and PoS first apply (August)	1989	1990	1990	1992
First statutory assessment (Summer)	1991	1994	1993	1994

THE ORDER FOR WALES

The Order for Wales is the same as for England, though it includes a brief appendix modifying the PoS for those pupils who are excepted from the National Curriculum requirements with regard to the teaching of English at KS1, having been taught wholly or partly through the medium of Welsh at KS1.

SPECIAL NOTE

In September 1992, the Secretaries of State announced a review of the English Order to be undertaken by NCC with CCW. The main aim of the review is to identify aspects of the English Order which require greater precision and clarity, while building on the strength of the current Order and avoiding over-prescription. New proposals for English are subject to statutory consultations. A revised Order is likely to take effect from August 1994 for pupils in KS1–3, and from 1995 for pupils beginning KS4. The current Order (summarised above) will remain in force until these dates.

WELSH

There are two models of Welsh in the National Curriculum:

Welsh (first language — core subject) and **Welsh second language (foundation subject).**

Normally Welsh second language will be introduced in KS1 but for some time there will be a considerable number of pupils beginning to study Welsh second language at the age of 11.

ATTAINMENT TARGETS

AT1	**Listening, viewing and speaking**	Pupils should be able to communicate effectively. They should be able to express themselves appropriately for various purposes among a variety of listeners, and they should be able to listen to language from various sources and respond and display understanding in word and action.
AT2	**Reading**	Pupils should be able to read in order to understand and respond to a variety of materials, and to gather information from different written sources.
AT3	**Writing**	Pupils should write effectively to convey meaning, information, opinion, feeling and imagination and adapt expression for different purposes and for different readers.

The ATs above are identical for both models.

For Welsh (core subject) there is a fourth AT — handwriting — which applies to KS1 only.

STRANDS

Welsh first language

AT1

1. Expressing personal/imaginative experiences
2. Discussing and expressing opinions
3. Conveying and exchanging information
4. Oral presentation
5. Awareness of features of oral language

AT2

1. Enjoyment of reading
2. Response to literary material
3. Response to non-literary material
4. Collecting information
5. Awareness of register and style

AT3

1. Personal/imaginative writing
2. Expressing opinions
3. Conveying information
4. Order and presentation
5. Awareness of conventions and style
6. Awareness of features of written language

Welsh second language

AT1

1. Understanding
2. Expressing personal/imaginative experiences
3. Conveying and exchanging information
4. Discussing and expressing opinions
5. Linguistic resources

AT2

1. Enjoyment of reading
2. Response to literary materials
3. Response to non-literary material

AT3

1. Personal/imaginative writing
2. Conveying information
3. Expressing opinions
4. Language resources

PROGRAMMES OF STUDY

For both models there is a PoS which relates to each AT and also to each key stage. However, the three skills are closely related and this is emphasised throughout.

The contents of the PoS are similar for both models but those for Welsh (core subject) have greater scope and depth and an increasing literary element. The PoS for pupils who begin to learn Welsh second language at age 11 are designed to reflect the pupils' greater maturity.

For Welsh second language at KS4 there are two PoS: Programme A for pupils who study Welsh second language as a single subject and Programme B for those studying Welsh second language as a short course. In Programme B the emphasis is on speaking and listening, whilst some reading and writing is undertaken in support of the oral element.

KEY STAGES/LEVELS

The full range of 10 levels applies to both models and also to those who begin to learn Welsh second language at age 11. There is provision of pupils who do exceptionally well at Welsh second language to transfer to the Welsh (core) course. This is dependent on facilities being available.

KS1	Levels 1–3
KS2	Levels 2–5
KS3	Levels 3–8
KS4	Levels 3–10

TIMETABLE

1. Schools where Welsh is currently taught	**KS1**	**KS2**	**KS3**	**KS4**
ATs and PoS first apply (August)	1990	1990	1990	1993
First statutory assessment (Summer)	1992	1994	1993	1995
2. Other schools	**KS1**	**KS2**	**KS3**	**KS4**
ATs and PoS first apply (August)	1992	1994	1992	1995
First statutory assessment (Summer)	1994	1998	1995	1997

SPECIAL NOTES

1. Some schools in certain anglicised areas where Welsh has not been hitherto studied have been granted an extended timetable for the introduction of Welsh second language.
2. A small number of schools have been given special dispensation to be exempt from teaching Welsh second language at KS4. This situation will be reviewed in 1996.
3. Pupils over the age of 13 are also exempted if they have not studied Welsh for at least one academic year in any of the preceeding three academic years. This is to exclude from compulsory Welsh those pupils moving into Wales or those already living in Wales who may transfer between a school where Welsh had not been taught to one where it is.

ATTAINMENT TARGETS

Design & technology capability		Aspects of design & technology
AT1	Identifying needs and opportunities	• Exploring and investigating contexts • Identifying and evaluating opportunities • Recognising issues and implications
AT2	Generating a design	• Exploring and developing ideas • Evaluating ideas and making decisions • Modelling and communication ideas
AT3	Planning and making	• Organising and planning • Using materials, equipment and processes • Making things work out
AT4	Evaluating	• Evaluating the outcomes and processes of one's own work • Evaluating the technological activity of other people, including those from other times and cultures

Information technology capability		Strands
AT5	Information technology capability	• Communicating ideas and information • Handling information • Designing, investigating, developing, exploring and evaluating models of real or imaginary situations • Measuring and controlling physical variables and movement • Understanding and evaluating the applications and effects of information technology

STRANDS

Key aspects of design & technology are shown above in relation to each AT. ATs 1–4 describe four complementary aspects of design & technology capability. Although the ATs appear to describe a sequential development, several aspects may be operating simultaneously at any time in a design & technology activity. The strands within AT5 are shown above. The **applications and effects of information technology** strand draws on the knowledge developed in the other four strands of information technology capability.

PROGRAMMES OF STUDY

The PoS for ATs 1–4 are in three parts.

1. For pupils in every key stage

Requirements are outlined on page 19 of the Order and include:

- designing and making artefacts, systems and environments;
- working in a range of contexts which includes home, school, recreation, community, business and industry;
- being careful for the safety of themselves and others;
- working with a range of materials, including textiles, graphic media, construction materials and food.

2. For pupils in a particular key stage

Requirements which apply to all pupils in that particular key stage are arranged in the following categories:

- developing and using artefacts, systems and environments;
- working with materials;
- developing and communicating ideas;
- satisfying needs and addressing opportunities.

3. For pupils working towards a particular level

Additional requirements (to 1 and 2 above) which apply to pupils working towards a particular level are arranged in the same categories as 2, above.

The PoS for AT5 are in three parts.

1. **General requirements for all key stages (page 51 of the Order)**
2. **Requirements for pupils in a particular key stage**
3. **Requirements for pupils working towards a particular level**

KEY STAGES/LEVELS

KS1	Levels 1–3
KS2	Levels 2–5
KS3	Levels 3–7
KS4	Levels 4–10

TIMETABLE

	KS1	**KS2**	**KS3**	**KS4**
ATs and PoS first apply (August)	1990	1990	1990	1993
First statutory assessment (Summer)	1992	1994	1993	1995

THE ORDER FOR WALES

The Order for Wales is the same as for England.

SPECIAL NOTES

1. Pupils' information technology capability will usually be developed through using information technology to support learning in other subject areas.
2. In June 1992, following advice from NCC and HMI, the Secretaries of State announced a review of the technology Order. AT5 (information technology capability) is unlikely to be affected by this review. NCC has recommended:
   - reducing the complexity and weight of the requirements, particularly at primary level;
   - introducing greater clarity and precision in the basic concepts, particularly in relation to practical skills;
   - introducing more flexibility and choice, particularly at secondary level;
   - strengthening the links to other Orders.

New proposals for technology are subject to statutory consultations. A revised Order is likely to take effect from August 1994 for pupils in KS1–3 and from 1995 for pupils beginning KS4. The current Order (summarised above) will remain in force until these dates.

HISTORY

ATTAINMENT TARGETS

AT1	**Knowledge and understanding of history**	The development of the ability to describe and explain historical change and cause, and analyse different features of historical situations.
AT2	**Interpretations of history**	The development of the ability to understand interpretations of history.
AT3	**The use of historical sources**	The development of pupils' ability to acquire evidence from historical sources and form judgements about their reliability and value.

STRANDS

AT1 has more SoA than ATs 2 and 3. This reflects the importance of the abilities defined in this AT. These are divided into three strands which can be traced upwards through the levels.

(i) **Change and continuity:** understanding that history is concerned with change, knowing about and distinguishing between different kinds of change.

(ii) **Causes and consequences:** knowing about and understanding the causes and consequences of historical events and developments.

(iii) **Knowing about and understanding:** the key features of past situations and the distinctive characteristics of past societies.

The first strand can be traced through Levels 1–7; the second through Levels 1–9 and the third through Levels 2–9. At Level 10 all three strands combine into a single strand of attainment.

RELATIONSHIP BETWEEN THE ATs AND PoS

Planning and teaching National Curriculum history involves thinking about the ATs and PoS simultaneously. Pupils can only meet the ATs by acquiring the knowledge of the historical content prescribed in the PoS. As they progress up the levels, pupils should be able to demonstrate a wider and deeper knowledge of the content in the PoS.

THE ORDER FOR WALES

Wales has a separate Order for history. Two features mark out the history curriculum in Wales — its content, reflected in the Order, and the perspectives which teachers should reflect in their planning and teaching. Within the PoS, prominence has been given to the history of Wales within an overall framework of British history. The teaching of history in Wales should, therefore, enable pupils to develop a sense of Wales' place in, and contribution to, the wider British, European and world contexts.

Whilst the content of the Orders is different, the structure of ATs and PoS is similar. Pages 38 and 39 show the differences between the PoS for England and Wales.

The PoS for history consist of two elements:

- general requirements which apply to all PoS;
- PoS for each key stage.

The general requirements contain important statements about the opportunities which should be provided in each study unit for the development of each AT. Pupils should also be enabled to explore links between history and other subjects; develop information technology capability, and the knowledge, understanding and skills related to cross-curricular themes. Provision should be made for pupils with special educational needs.

The PoS should enable pupils to develop knowledge and understanding of British, European and world history.

The PoS for each key stage consist of four sections:

- **key elements,** such as concepts to be taught and types of historical sources to be included;
- **opportunities** pupils need to meet the ATs;
- the methods by which pupils can **find out about the past** and **communicate the results** of their investigations;
- **study units** to be taught.

STUDY UNITS

At KS1 there is one study unit which must be taught throughout the key stage.

At KS2–4 the PoS are made up of:

- **core study units;**
- **supplementary study units** which complement or extend the core.

At KS2 pupils should be taught nine study units. At KS3 pupils should be taught all five core and three supplementary study units. At KS4 pupils will be able to follow one of two courses. Model 1 contains a core study unit and is designed to be taught as a short course on its own or in combination with another subject. Model 2 is an extended course and is designed to fulfil the requirements for a GCSE qualification in history.

PROGRAMME OF STUDY (WALES)

The PoS for history consist of two elements:

- general requirements which apply to all PoS;
- PoS for each key stage.

The general requirements describe the important principles which underlie the study of history. These include developing an understanding of chronology, the diversity of society, and the experiences of men, women and children. It also involves viewing the past through a range of perspectives and at a variety of levels. Opportunities should be provided to make links between history and other subjects, and particularly with the geography, languages and cultures of Wales and to promote cross-curricular themes and competences. Provision should be made for pupils with special educational needs.

The PoS for each key stage consist of three sections:

- **a general introduction,** indicating which study units must be taught;
- **general requirements,** indicating the types of historical sources to be included, the concepts and terms to be taught and the opportunities which pupils should have to investigate the past and communicate their understanding;
- **opportunities** pupils need to meet the ATs.

STUDY UNITS

At KS1 there is one study unit which must be taught throughout the key stage.

At KS2 pupils must be taught eight study units.

At KS3 pupils must be taught four compulsory units which must be delivered sequentially, a local history unit and two supplementary units.

At KS4 pupils will be able to follow one of two courses. Model A consists of two study units and is designed to be taught as a short course on its own or in combination with another subject. Model B is an extended course and is designed to fulfil the requirements for a GCSE or equivalent qualification in history.

KEY STAGES/LEVELS

KS1	Levels 1–3
KS2	Levels 2–5
KS3	Levels 3–7
KS4	Levels 4–10

TIMETABLE

	KS1	**KS2**	**KS3**	**KS4**
ATs and PoS first apply (August)	1991	1991	1991	1994
First statutory assessment (Summer)	1993	1995	1994	1996

GEOGRAPHY

ATTAINMENT TARGETS

	ATs		Strands
Skills	**AT1**	**Geographical skills**	The use of maps and fieldwork techniques.
Places	**AT2**	**Knowledge and understanding of places**	The distinctive features, similarities and differences between places in local, regional, national and international contexts; the relationships between themes and issues in particular locations.
Themes	**AT3**	**Physical geography**	Weather and climate; landforms such as rivers, river basins, seas and oceans; vegetation; animals and soils.
	AT4	**Human geography**	Population, settlements, communications and movements; economic activities.
	AT5	**Environmental geography**	The use and misuse of natural resources; the quality and vulnerability of different environments; the possibilities for protecting and managing environments.

Physical, human and environmental geography are referred to in the Order as **Themes.**

STRANDS

Within each AT, SoA can be grouped into strands of linked content as shown above.

PROGRAMMES OF STUDY

There is a PoS which corresponds to each key stage. Each PoS is divided into five sections which correspond to the five ATs.

Geographical skills – AT1

An enquiry approach and fieldwork should be undertaken where appropriate, along with opportunities to use information technology.

Places and Themes – ATs 2–5

Each key stage PoS is further divided into:

- a PoS for all pupils in the key stage;
- a PoS for pupils working towards the highest levels of attainment in the key stage.

AT2 offers pupils opportunities to study specified places which are important in their own right. It also provides logical contexts in which to develop aspects of the thematic studies required for ATs 3, 4 and 5. The Order sets out a minimum requirement for knowledge about the British Isles, Europe and the world in the form of a series of maps. Geographical skills (AT1) should be integrated into all geography work and not taught in isolation.

At KS4 pupils may follow a short course in geography which consists of a selection of the content from the full course. Content is specified by a reduced number of SoA in ATs, 1 2 and 5 and a choice of strands from ATs 3 and 4.

KEY STAGES/LEVELS

KS1	Levels 1–3
KS2	Levels 2–5
KS3	Levels 3–7
KS4	Levels 4–10

TIMETABLE

	KS1	KS2	KS3	KS4
ATs and PoS first apply (August)	1991	1991	1991	1994
Statutory assessment (Summer)	1993	1995	1994	1996

THE ORDER FOR WALES

Separate Orders exist for geography in England and Wales. The basic structure and content of the Orders are the same. However, the Order for Wales specifies the pupils' Home Region as Wales, and uses many Welsh examples in the non-statutory examples given in the PoS and SoA. There is an additional map, Map G: Wales.

MODERN FOREIGN LANGUAGES

ATTAINMENT TARGETS

AT1	**Listening**	The development of pupils' ability to understand and respond to spoken language.
AT2	**Speaking**	The development of pupils' ability to communicate in speech.
AT3	**Reading**	The development of pupils' ability to read, understand and respond to written language.
AT4	**Writing**	The development of pupils' ability to communicate in writing.

STRANDS

The main strands of progression as they relate to the ATs in modern foreign languages are:

- **Range and complexity of language and texts** (ATs 1 and 3);
- **Understanding/response** (ATs 1 and 3);
- **Range and complexity of language and tasks** (ATs 2 and 4);
- **Quality of communication** (ATs 2 and 4).
- **Independence** (ATs 2, 3 and 4);

PROGRAMMES OF STUDY

The PoS at KS3 and KS4 consist of two parts, prefaced by general requirements which apply to both key stages.

General requirements – contain important statements about the use of the target language for real purposes, in which language skills are combined; opportunities for developing information technology capability; and provision for pupils with special educational needs.

Part I – **Learning and using the target language:** the skills which should be developed, and opportunities which should be provided, through activities in the target language. These are grouped under six section headings.

1. Communicating in the target language
2. Understanding and responding
3. Developing language learning skills and awareness of language
4. Developing cultural awareness
5. Developing the ability to work with others
6. Developing the ability to learn independently

Part II	– **Areas of experience (AoE):** the content and contexts for learning and using a modern foreign language set out as seven AoE which should be explored through the target language. Area A: Everyday Activities Area B: Personal and Social Life Area C: The World Around Us Area D: The World of Education, Training and Work Area E: The World of Communications Area F: The International World Area G: The World of Imagination and Creativity

Pupils should have opportunities through the AoE to explore links with other subjects and develop knowledge, understanding and skills related to cross-curricular dimensions and themes.

Parts I and II of the PoS should be taught together. Alongside the opportunities set out in PoS Part I in the Order are boxes which indicate the ATs to which the PoS statements relate.

The full course in modern foreign languages has a PoS called Model A as defined above. Pupils who do not follow the full course leading to a single subject GCSE (or equivalent) at KS4 are required to select, for assessment purposes, a minimum of two ATs. For this course they follow a reduced PoS called Model B which consists of the General requirements, the whole of PoS Part II and a selection from PoS Part I relating to the ATs chosen.

KEY STAGES/LEVELS

The full range of 10 levels applies to both KS3 and KS4. The 10-level scale would normally be expected to cover a five-year learning period. Most pupils are expected to make rapid progress through the early levels which also offer lower attaining pupils or those with special educational needs worthwhile and realisable goals. Progression becomes a somewhat steeper path in the middle to upper levels, which present challenges to all pupils. The highest levels are appropriate to very able and bilingual pupils.

TIMETABLE

	KS3	**KS4**
ATs and PoS first apply (August)	1992	1995
First statutory assessment (Summer)	1995	1997

THE ORDER FOR WALES

The Order for Wales is the same as for England.

SPECIAL NOTE

The Section 3 Order specifies the 19 modern foreign languages which count as National Curriculum languages. These are the eight official languages of the European Community (EC) (Danish, Dutch, French, German, Modern Greek, Italian, Portuguese and Spanish) and 11 other languages of commercial and cultural importance [Arabic, Bengali, Chinese (Cantonese or Mandarin), Gujarati, Modern Hebrew, Hindi, Japanese, Panjabi, Russian, Turkish and Urdu]. Schools must offer at least one of the official EC languages as a foundation subject.

ART

ATTAINMENT TARGETS (ENGLAND)

AT1	**Investigating and making**	The development of visual perception and the skills associated with investigating and making in art, craft and design.
AT2	**Knowledge and understanding**	The development of visual literacy and knowledge and understanding of art, craft and design including the history of art, our diverse artistic heritage and a variety of other artistic traditions, together with the ability to make practical connections between this and pupils' own work.

STRANDS (ENGLAND)

Each end of key stage statement relates to a strand of progression.

AT1

- Recording what has been seen, imagined or remembered: visual perception
- Gathering and using resources and materials
- Using different materials and techniques in practical work
- Reviewing and modifying work

AT2

- Knowledge of different kinds of art and the development of visual literacy
- Knowledge of different periods, cultures and traditions in art, and the work of influential artists
- Applying knowledge of the work of other artists to their own work

PROGRAMMES OF STUDY (ENGLAND)

There are two parts to the PoS: specific key stage requirements and more general requirements which apply throughout the three key stages. These general requirements establish some vital ground rules on the importance of:

- balance between art, craft and design;
- planning which takes account of previous achievement;
- varied methods of working, individually, in groups and as a whole class;
- working in two and three dimensions on a variety of scales;
- appropriate use of information technology;
- evaluation by pupils of their own and others' work;
- art from a variety of cultures, Western and non-Western.

The specific requirements for each key stage are set out in relation to each AT.

Each PoS statement relates to an end of key stage statement and is illustrated by non-statutory examples.

ATTAINMENT TARGETS (WALES)

AT1	**Understanding**	Pupils should develop the ability to evaluate and respond practically and imaginatively to the approaches of others, including artists, craftworkers and designers working in diverse contemporary and historical cultures and contexts.
AT2	**Making**	Pupils should develop the skills and knowledge involved in the process of making (including the ability to select, control and experiment with materials, tools and techniques and an understanding of the visual language of art, craft and design) and be able to apply these in their own work to develop, express and modify their ideas, intentions and feelings.
AT3	**Investigating**	Pupils should develop their visual perception, recording from direct observation, memory and the imagination and be able to visualise ideas drawing on a wide range of resources which they have selected from the natural and made environment.

STRANDS (WALES)

Each end of key stage statement relates to a strand of progression.

AT1

- Using knowledge of the work of other artists, craftworkers and designers in their own work.
- Evaluating the work of others, including artists, craftworkers and designers working in various contemporary and historical cultures and contexts.

AT2

- Applying knowledge of the visual language of art and the skills of making with materials, tools and techniques in practical work.
- Reviewing and modifying their work.

AT3

- Recording images, ideas or feelings which have been observed, imagined or remembered.
- Collecting and organising visual and other resources with which to develop an idea or theme.

PROGRAMMES OF STUDY (WALES)

There are two parts to the PoS: specific key stage requirements and more general requirements which apply throughout the three key stages.

These general requirements establish some vital ground rules on the importance of:

- balance between art, craft and design;
- planning which takes account of previous achievement;
- working individually, in groups and as a whole class;
- working in two and three dimensions and on a variety of scales;
- appropriate use of information technology;
- learning about artists, craftworkers and designers working in various times, cultures, contexts and materials;
- the study of works of art, craft and design including local and Welsh examples.

The specific requirements for each key stage are set out in relation to each AT.

Each PoS statement relates to an end of key stage statement and is illustrated by non-statutory examples.

KEY STAGES/LEVELS

There is not a statutory 10-level framework for art. For KS1–3, end of key stage statements define the knowledge, skills and understanding which pupils of different abilities and maturities can be expected to achieve by the end of each key stage. Programmes of study at KS4 are non-statutory.

TIMETABLE

	KS1	KS2	KS3	KS4
ATs and PoS first apply (August)	1992	1992	1992	1995*
First statutory assessment (Summer)	1994	1996	1995	1997*

* KS4 is non-statutory. In England the great majority of schools are expected to offer art to pupils who wish to continue their study of the subject after 14. In Wales, pupils should be able to take art **or** music in KS4.

MUSIC

ATTAINMENT TARGETS (ENGLAND)

AT1	**Performing and composing**	The development of the ability to perform and compose music with understanding.
AT2	**Listening and appraising**	The development of the ability to listen to and appraise music, including knowledge of musical history, our diverse musical heritage, and a variety of other musical traditions.

STRANDS (ENGLAND)

Each end of key stage statement relates to a strand of progression.

AT1 has five strands: the first three are linked to performing; the remaining two are linked to composing.

- Playing and singing (by ear, from signs and notations)
- Controlling sounds made by the voice and a range of musical instruments
- Performing with others
- Composing, arranging and improvising
- Refining, recording and communicating musical ideas

AT2 has three strands.

- Listening and identifying musical elements and structures
- The history of music: its composers and traditions
- Appraising music: appreciation of live and recorded music

In KS1 the second and third strands are combined in AT1, and the first and second strands are combined in AT2, making a total of six end of key stage statements.

ATTAINMENT TARGETS (WALES)

AT1	**Performing**	Pupils should develop the skills and competences needed to perform, using voices and instruments, their own compositions and those of others in a variety of styles. They should be able to respond to appropriate signs, symbols, cues and instructions in doing so, and should also be able to present their performances with commitment, enjoyment and skill.
AT2	**Composing**	Pupils should develop the skills and competences needed to devise musical compositions and arrangements and to improvise. They should be able to record their ideas (work in progress, as well as finished compositions) by appropriate means. Composing may include improvising and arranging.
AT3	**Appraising**	Pupils should develop the skills and knowledge needed, as audience listeners, to respond to the elements of music from a wide range of styles and from different cultural traditions; to make reasoned judgements about and evaluate performances and compositions; and to bring to bear, in doing so, relevant knowledge of the historical and cultural background of the music concerned.

STRANDS (WALES)

Each end of key stage statement relates to a strand of progression.

AT1

- Playing and singing by ear, from signs and notations
- Performing with others
- Controlling sounds made by voice and instruments
- Performing a solo part

AT2

- Exploring, selecting and organising sounds to develop musical ideas
- Refining, completing and storing compositions

AT3

- Listening attentively to music and responding to musical elements
- Discussing and evaluating music

PROGRAMMES OF STUDY (ENGLAND)

There are two parts to the PoS: general statutory requirements for all key stages and specific requirements for each key stage.

General requirements define:

- the opportunities which should be given to pupils throughout all the key stages;
- the range of repertoire for listening and performing.

Although the PoS have been set out in relation to each AT, there is no implication that teaching activities or learning opportunities should be designed to address them separately. Each PoS statement relates to an end of key stage statement and is illustrated by non-statutory examples.

PROGRAMMES OF STUDY (WALES)

There are two parts to the PoS: general statutory requirements for all key stages and specific requirements for each key stage.

General requirements:

- the opportunities which should be given to pupils throughout all the key stages;
- the range of repertoire for listening and performing, with specific reference to the music of Wales.

Although the PoS have been set out in relation to each AT, there is no implication that teaching activities or learning opportunities should be designed to address them separately.

Each PoS statement relates to an end of key stage statement and is illustrated by non-statutory examples.

KEY STAGES/LEVELS

There is not a statutory 10-level framework for music. For KS1–3, end of key stage statements define the knowledge, skills and understanding which pupils of different abilities and maturities are expected to achieve by the end of each key stage. Programmes of study at KS4 are non-statutory.

TIMETABLE

	KS1	KS2	KS3	KS4
ATs and PoS first apply (August)	1992	1992	1992	1995*
First statutory assessment (Summer)	1994	1996	1995	1997*

* KS4 is non-statutory. In England the great majority of schools are expected to offer music to pupils who wish to continue their study of the subject after 14. In Wales, pupils should be able to take music **or** art in KS4.

PHYSICAL EDUCATION

ATTAINMENT TARGETS

There is only one AT for physical education

STRANDS

The single AT for physical education encompasses the strands of planning, performing and evaluating whilst retaining progression in aspects of health-related exercise. Progression can be traced through the strands in the end of key stage statements across the key stages.

PROGRAMMES OF STUDY

The PoS consist of three parts.

1. **General requirements relating to PoS**

   These requirements should apply to all key stages and be taught through all areas of activity.

2. **Programmes of study (general)**

   These set out what must be taught to pupils during each key stage in order to meet the objectives set out in the end of key stage statements.

3. **Programmes of study (activity specific)**

   Six areas of activity are defined:

   - athletic activities;
   - dance;
   - games:
   - gymnastic activities;
   - outdoor and adventurous activities;
   - swimming.

Requirements relating to the areas of activity vary according to key stage.

Key Stages 1 and 2

All six areas of activity should be experienced, but at KS1 and KS2 emphasis should be on dance, games and gymnastic activities. All pupils should be be able to swim at least 25 metres unaided and demonstrate an understanding of water safety by the end of KS2. If swimming is taught during KS1 pupils should start the KS2 swimming programme at the appropriate point. The provision relating to swimming will come into effect from August 1994.

Key Stage 3

Pupils should pursue the PoS for a **minimum** of four areas of activity,, with games compulsory each year (swimming having been incorporated into other areas of activity).

Key Stage 4

At least two activities should be experienced either from the same area of activity or from two different areas.

KEY STAGES/LEVELS

There is not a 10-level framework for physical education. However, at KS4 some sort of level framework will be devised for the purpose of GCSE.

TIMETABLE

	KS1	KS2	KS3	KS4
ATs and PoS first apply (August)	1992	1992	1992	1995
First statutory assessment (Summer)	1994	1996	1995	1997

THE ORDER FOR WALES

The Order for Wales is the same as for England.

RELIGIOUS EDUCATION IN THE BASIC CURRICULUM IN ENGLAND AND WALES

The legal position

Religious education has been a compulsory element in the schooling of all pupils since 1944, and this requirement was reinforced by ERA.

The *Education Act 1944* and ERA

- Religious education is included in the basic curriculum for all registered pupils 4–19 in maintained schools (ERA 1.8.2).
- At the request of a parent, any child in a maintained school must be excused from receiving religious education. Teachers may also withdraw from teaching religious education.
- Every LEA shall have a Standard Advisory Council for religious education (SACRE) which will **advise** the LEA on matters related to religious education and collective worship. SACREs have the power to require the LEA to set up an Agreed Syllabus Conference.
- Any new Agreed Syllabus must reflect the fact that the religious traditions of Great Britain are in the main Christian, but it must also include teaching about the other principal world religions represented in Great Britain.
- Religious education teaching in maintained schools must follow the Agreed Syllabus for the LEA, produced by an Agreed Syllabus Conference.*
- Religious education must not seek to convert pupils, or seek to impose on them any particular religion or denomination.* (1944 Act, Section 26)

It is by maintaining a balance between these two areas that religious education is generally seen as contributing to the spiritual, moral, cultural and intellectual development of pupils.

* This does not apply to aided and special agreement schools.

DES/WO guidance

Circular 3/89 (Religious Education and Collective Worship)

- When drawing up an Agreed Syllabus, the Agreed Syllabus Conference (representatives from the Church of England, other Christian denominations, other religions, teachers, elected members) should assume that there will be a reasonable time available for the study of religious education, and that religious education has equal standing with core and foundation subjects (111.20).
- The Secretary of State hopes that Conferences will consider fully the possibility of recommending the inclusion of locally agreed ATs, PoS and assessment arrangements. (111.20).
- Conferences are free to devise and seek approval for their own syllabuses for GCSE.

Letter from DES to all Chief Education Officers 18 March 1991

The content of an Agreed Syllabus should:

- be based on the traditions, practices and teaching of Christianity and the other principal world religions;
- extend beyond information about religions and religious traditions, practices and teaching, to wider areas of morality and consideration of how religious beliefs and practices affect peoples' daily lives;
- have regard to the national as well as the local position and population.

AGREED SYLLABUSES DEVELOPED SINCE 1988

Aims of religious education

Most Agreed Syllabuses include two broad aims for religious education. These are that pupils should:

- understand the teachings and practices of Christianity and the other world religions;
- be encouraged to develop their own beliefs and values.

It is by maintaining a balance between these two areas that religious education is generally seen as contributing to the spiritual, moral, cultural and intellectual development of pupils.

Attainment targets and programmes of study in religious education

Many of the Agreed Syllabuses written since ERA include ATs and PoS, but there is no statutory requirement to do so. In some syllabuses ATs are based on areas of content, such as 'beliefs', 'worship and celebrations' or 'lifestyle'. Others, however, have followed the National Curriculum history model by having a few process-based ATs which are applied to all the content in the PoS. These ATs include, for example, 'interpretations of expressions of religion', 'evaluation, knowledge and understanding of religious belief and practice' and 'application of religion to the lives of individuals and societies'.

THE FOCUS OF RELIGIOUS EDUCATION

Concepts in religious education

Agreed Syllabuses are devised locally. Although the religions studied vary from LEA to LEA, as does the balance between the teaching of Christianity and other religions, there are a number of central concepts and issues which appear to different degrees in most syllabuses. These include, for example, beliefs about God, founders of religions, sacred texts, worship and meditation, festivals, rites of passage, religious beliefs, ethical teachings and the rules of religions.

Attitudes in religious education

Certain attitudes are generally encouraged in religious education. These include, for example, curiosity, self-confidence and self-esteem, respect for the views and ways of life of others, open-mindedness, critical ability and consideration for others.

Questions and issues in religious education

Religious education in most syllabuses seeks to address the questions which are of universal human concern. These include, for example, Who am I? Why am I here? Why did the universe begin? What is the purpose of life? Do human beings have a soul? What happens after death? In considering these questions, pupils will normally consider the responses of the religions they are studying.

NCC advice on religious education

- Where possible pupils should take a religious studies course to GCSE.
- The quality of religious teaching should match that in other National Curriculum subjects.
- Where appropriate, work in religious education should be assessed and reported.

PART THREE: FURTHER INFORMATION AND GUIDANCE ABOUT THE CURRICULUM AND ASSESSMENT

1. NCC PUBLICATIONS

NCC publications can be divided into various categories according to the type of information they contain. These categories are as follows.

GENERAL

These general publications aim to provide background information on the National Curriculum and news of current developments and initiatives.

NCC News
The NCC Newsletter has now been replaced by a joint newsletter from DFE, NCC and SEAC but back copies of issues 3–7 are still available while stocks last. The last issue (No. 7) was autumn 1991.

Corporate literature
NCC's *Corporate Plan 1992–95* (1991) and a brochure entitled *National Curriculum Council* (1991) give detailed information on NCC's work, its remit and function.

Circulars
Short summaries of reports, such as NCC's report on *Monitoring the Implementation of the National Curriculum Core Subjects: 1989–90* (1991), are available in the form of circulars.

Posters
Useful for wall display, NCC's posters cover drama and the ATs and PoS in technology.

NON-STATUTORY GUIDANCE

Designed for teachers to slot into the back of the National Curriculum subject ringbinders, non-statutory guidance (NSG) is published after the statutory Order. NSG is intended to help teachers understand and implement the requirements of the National Curriculum. It focuses on aspects of school policy, planning and classroom practice.

INSET RESOURCES

Primarily training materials for teachers, although some would be of interest to governors, NCC's INSET resources may be in print or video format and cover a variety of different subject areas. Some are applicable to particular key stages, e.g. *Implementing Design & Technology at Key Stages 1 and 2* (1991) and *Mathematics Programmes of Study: INSET for Key Stages 3 and 4* (1991/2).

CURRICULUM GUIDANCE

The series covers primary education, special educational needs, the whole curriculum and the five cross-curricular themes.

CONSULTATION REPORTS

These are summaries of the views expressed during statutory consultation in each National Curriculum subject area. They are eventually superseded by the draft Order and final statutory Order but are useful to trace the historical development of a National Curriculum subject from working group to final Order.

ECONOMIC AND INDUSTRIAL UNDERSTANDING PUBLICATIONS

These are publications which consider teacher placements in industry as a way of helping National Curriculum implementation, work experience for pupils, and planning how to develop economic and industrial understanding in the curriculum. There are also subject INSET packs for most subjects at KS3 and KS4.

OTHER PUBLICATIONS

Further publications on aspects such as religious education, KS4 and monitoring and evaluation are available from NCC. See current publications list and order form for details.

A full list of NCC publications and prices is available from NCC Information Office at the following address:

National Curriculum Council
Information Office
Albion Wharf
25 Skeldergate
York
YO1 2XL
Tel: (0904) 622533

2. CCW PUBLICATIONS

The following publications are available from CCW. They are available in English, Welsh or bilingual versions. Like publications from NCC, they can be divided into categories which are explained below.

CORPORATE LITERATURE

The annual report and corporate plan of the Council give a background to the work and objectives of CCW.

THE CCW NEWSLETTER

This is published on a termly basis and aims to keep the profession informed about the developments in the National Curriculum and about CCW's work and position.

ADVISORY PAPERS

Whenever the Secretary of State for Wales asks CCW for advice on the shape of National Curriculum subject Orders, the Council consults the profession in Wales before replying to him. The text of this advice is subsequently published as an Advisory Paper, which has a short life time as draft and final subject Orders soon follow.

POLICY DOCUMENTS

These documents are restricted to areas/issues on which the Council feels a need to publish specific guidance in the name of the council. They fall into the category of material which is distributed free to all schools in Wales and are available in both English and Welsh.

WORKING DOCUMENTS

These short-life documents are occasional papers which focus on specific topics and are available in English only. They are distributed free to schools serving the relevant key stage.

CURRICULUM BULLETINS

These are short statements, sometimes topical such as *Curriculum Bulletin 2: Geography in the National Curriculum in Wales* (1989), but also explanatory such as *Curriculum Bulletin 6: Developing Whole-School Policies for Pupils with Special Educational Needs* (1992).

NON-STATUTORY GUIDANCE

CCW publishes non-statutory guidance (NSG) for each National Curriculum subject to accompany the Orders in their ring binders. CCW and NCC may work collaboratively on the initial development of NSG but CCW's NSG will reflect the particular needs of teachers in Wales, Council's own position, and the differences that may exist between the subject Orders for England and for Wales (i.e. in history and geography, art and music). In addition, CCW has produced NSG for Welsh and Welsh Second Language to accompany the Order for Welsh. NSG is published in English and Welsh versions.

Teacher Support Programme Publications

CCW has involved teachers in considering a range of identified issues, and is drawing on their experience of implementing the National Curriculum. The programme embraces both National Curriculum subjects and cross-curricular themes. New publications in the series are automatically sent to subscribers.

For more information about publications, subscription or the work of the Council contact:

Curriculum Council for Wales
Castle Buildings
Womanby Street
Cardiff CF1 9SX
Tel: (0222) 344946

3. SEAC PUBLICATIONS

SEAC publishes information on all aspects of assessment, recording and reporting.

GENERAL

The SEAC newsletter *SEAC Recorder* has been replaced by a joint newsletter from NCC, DFE and SEAC called *Schools Update* but back issues are available while stocks last.

SEAC also produces National Curriculum support materials which are designed to be of use to teachers in schools and to providers of in-service and initial training. There are three types of material.

SPECIFIC INFORMATION RELATING TO END OF KEY STAGE PROCEDURES

School assessment folders

These contain information about end of key stage task/test and teacher assessment requirements. These are usually issued early in the final year of a key stage.

Exemplification of pupils' work assessed

This material shows examples of how and why judgements have been made about pupils' attainment. The purpose is to support teachers in making judgements about their own pupils' work in relation to the statements of attainments and attainment targets and to contribute to a nationally consistent interpretation of standards.

Exemplification of teacher assessment in practice

This material shows examples of how different teachers and schools are managing different aspects of assessment as part of their normal classroom practice. Its purpose is not to present definitive models but rather to include examples from which teachers can draw in order to develop their own practice.

GCSE CHIEF EXAMINERS' CONFERENCE REPORTS

These reports, which are available in a variety of subjects, present the findings of annual conferences of chief examiners and chief moderators from each GCSE examining group in relation to a particular theme. Treatment of the theme comes substantially from a detailed appraisal of all the GCSE papers in the subject from the previous year's examination.

GCSE AND A/AS GENERAL SCRUTINY REPORTS

These annual reports present a general picture of the findings of particular scrutiny exercises during the year in question. The General Scrutiny Reports cover the findings under specific headings, e.g. Coursework, Question Papers, Mark Schemes, etc. The reports provide a means of disseminating the findings of a range of individual scrutinies in a general way between examining groups and boards to give a picture of current thinking and practice in GCSE and A/AS examining.

EVALUATION AND MONITORING UNIT PUBLICATIONS

Titles of Evaluation and Monitoring Units (EMU) publications include the *Assessment Matters* series, e.g. No. 4 *Language for Learning* (1991). The publications present and interpret evidence from surveys of pupils' performance in relation to the particular area covered by each document.

SEAC publications are available using pro-forma response forms sent periodically to schools.

Further information may be obtained from:

SEAC Information
Newcombe House
45 Notting Hill Gate
London
W11 3JB
Tel: 071 229 1234

4. DFE AND WELSH OFFICE PUBLICATIONS

The following publications are produced by DFE and WOED. Publications in Wales are available in English and Welsh.

NATIONAL CURRICULUM STATUTORY ORDERS

The Orders contain attainment targets and programmes of study and are issued in a ringbinder. These can be purchased from Her Majesty's Stationery Office (HMSO) and NCC. In Wales, English and Welsh language versions of the statutory Orders are available. These include separate Orders for history, geography, art and music which reflect the Welsh culture and traditions. These can be purchased from HMSO.

SCHOOLS UPDATE

This is a termly newsletter from DFE, NCC and SEAC for schools teachers and governors.

DISCUSSION PAPERS

In January 1992 the DES published *Curriculum Organisation and Classroom Practice in Primary Schools: A Discussion Paper*. In Wales, HMI Wales published *Classroom Organisation and Teaching Methods*. Both discussion papers contain much that is relevant to the National Curriculum.

STATUTORY INSTRUMENTS

These provide legislation on various aspects of education in England and Wales, e.g. *(Education) Information on School Examination Results (England) Regulations 1991* (SI No. 1991/1265).

CIRCULARS

These are free leaflets on a variety of educational issues. A circular accompanies each new statutory Order to provide guidance on the implementation of the attainment targets and programmes of study. These circulars also outline the broad framework for the assessment of pupils' work. Separate circulars are issued by DFE and WOED.

PROPOSALS OF THE SECRETARY OF STATE FOR EDUCATION AND SCIENCE AND THE SECRETARY OF STATE FOR WALES

Obtainable free from NCC (and WOED for students in Wales), while stocks last, these documents contain the initial proposals of the Secretaries of State for the content of each National Curriculum subject. These are superseded by NCC's and CCW's consultation reports in each subject and eventually by the final statutory Orders.

GENERAL GUIDES

Current titles include *Your Child and the National Curriculum: a Parent's Guide to What is Happening in Schools*; *How is Your child Doing at School?* and *Your Child's Report: What it Means and How it Can Help*. These are available in English, Welsh, and eight other languages (Bengali, Chinese, Greek, Gujarati, Hindi, Panjabi, Turkish and Urdu).

Free publications are available from:

DFE
Publications Centre
PO Box 2193
London
E15 2EU
Tel: 081 533 2000

Schools Curriculum Division
WOED
Phase II
Government Buildings
Ty Glas Road
Llanishen
Cardiff CF4 5WE
Tel: 0222 761456

Priced publications are available from:

HMSO
PO Box 276
London
SW8 5DT
Tel: 071 873 9090 (orders)
Tel: 071 873 0011 (enquiries)

HMSO Bookshop
Senghennydd Road
Cathays
Cardiff CF2 4AG
Tel: 0222 228779

5. HMI PUBLICATIONS

Each year several hundred Her Majesty's Inspectorate (HMI) inspection and survey reports are published by the DFE and WOED. These contain evidence and evaluative comment relevant to schools' preparedness for, and implementation of, the National Curriculum.

For details of titles, check with HMSO and DFE for English publications (see above addresses) and with HMI Wales for the Welsh titles.

HMI Wales
Welsh Office Education Department
Phase II
Government Buildings
Ty Glas Road
Llanishem
Cardiff CF4 5WE
Tel: 0222 761456

The kinds of report **HMI England** produce are:

EDUCATION OBSERVED

This is a series of some 20 publications. Recent titles relevant to the National Curriculum include *The Implementation of The Curricular Requirements of ERA: An Overview by HM Inspectorate on the First Year 1989-90* and *Special Needs Issues: A Survey by HMI*. These are available from HMSO.

PUBLICATIONS RELATING TO PRIMARY EDUCATION

Recent titles include *Teaching and Learning of Drama* and *Teaching and Learning of Physical Education*. They are available from HMSO.

PUBLICATIONS RELATING TO NATIONAL CURRICULUM IMPLEMENTATION

Various reports on implementation of the National Curriculum subjects, e.g. *English Key Stages 1,2, and 3* (1992). They are available from HMSO.

OTHER REPORTS

These are available on a variety of issues, e.g. *Education in England 1990-91* (1992) and *Geography in the Early Years* (1991). Most are available free from DFE Publications Centre.

The kinds of report **HMI Wales** produce are:

REPORTS OF INSPECTIONS

These are of individual institutions and of local and national surveys of aspects of education.

OCCASIONAL PAPERS

These are on topics such as *Poetry in the Primary School, Coursework in the GCSE, Assessment and Monitoring of Pupils' Progress in KS3.*

6. IN SERVICE EDUCATION AND TRAINING (INSET)

Serving teachers will receive further training in the National Curriculum and assessment, during their induction period and afterwards. The nature, content and duration of that training will depend on their responsibilities, their needs and the wider needs of the schools in which they teach. There is a wide range of training and materials available.

The National Curriculum is intended to improve the quality of teaching and learning for all pupils. It is not therefore a 'once-for-all' exercise but rather one that is continually monitored and evaluated, by NCC, CCW, SEAC, HMI and others. It relies for its development on feedback from teachers and schools.

Now that the framework of the National Curriculum is in place, it is no surprise that attention is increasingly focused on how it is working in practice, what the long-term future implications are going to be, and what measures need to be taken to anticipate them.

Questions to be asked and issues to be addressed include the following.

RAISING STANDARDS

Are teaching objectives in the different subjects of the National Curriculum pitched at an appropriately challenging level? How do we compare with other countries?

Is the curriculum as a whole (as laid down in ERA) preparing pupils for adult life?

Do the National Curriculum Orders contribute to the spiritual, moral, cultural, mental and physical development of pupils as ERA requires?

Are the foundation subjects, together with the locally agreed syllabuses for religious education, meeting the requirements of the Act?

MANAGEABILITY

Does the weight of detail, structure of programmes of study, attainment targets and statements of attainment need attention?

How are assessment procedures affecting curriculum practice?

Does the current level of prescription prevent teachers from exercising their professional judgement in matching the curriculum to the particular needs of their pupils?

THE PRIMARY CURRICULUM

Does the National Curriculum give sufficient emphasis at Key Stage 1 to the basics of reading, writing, spelling and arithmetic to ensure a good foundation for subsequent learning?

How can primary teachers acquire the knowledge, skills and understanding needed to teach the range demanded by the National Curriculum?

Which are the best ways to manage and organise the National Curriculum in Key Stages 1 and 2?

How may continuity and progression between infant and junior, primary and secondary best be achieved, given the very different approaches to teaching?

Does the National Curriculum cater appropriately for the different stages of development of pupils entering school for the first time?

What issues does the implementation of the National Curriculum raise for very small primary schools?

KEY STAGE 4 AND BEYOND

What opportunities does the flexibility at Key Stage 4 provide for developing worthwhile combinations of subjects while ensuring curriculum coherence?

Which National Curriculum Orders offer the greatest scope for the development of combined and vocationally related courses pre-16 with continuity and progression post-16?

> As evidence emerges, NCC, CCW and SEAC may make recommendations to the Secretaries of State about how the content of foundation subjects or assessment arrangements might be revised in the interests of raising standards and/or manageability. In doing so, it will be important to balance the needs of continuity and change. Changes will only be recommended if they are essential to achieving the objectives of ERA.

APPENDIX: KEY TERMS, CONCEPTS AND ABBREVIATIONS

Assessment arrangements – arrangements, specified by the Secretaries of State, for assessing pupils' attainment in each National Curriculum subject.

Attainment targets (ATs) – objectives for each foundation subject, setting out the knowledge, skills and understanding that pupils of different abilities and maturities are expected to develop within that subject area.

Basic Curriculum – this comprises the National Curriculum and religious education.

Breadth – associated also with balance; implies a curriculum which comprises a range and balance of subjects and cross-curricular elements.

CAAW – Curriculum and Assessment Authority for Wales, see page 10.

CCW – Curriculum Council for Wales.

Combined course – a combination of two short courses in foundation and/or non-foundation subjects.

Continuity – the planned provision of teaching, learning and other experiences which facilitate pupils' continuous development.

Core subjects – mathematics, science and English and, for schools in Wales which are Welsh-speaking schools, Welsh.

Cross-curricular elements – the dimensions, skills and themes identified by NCC as contributing to the **Whole Curriculum. CCW** has identified a similar set of matters which schools need to consider in their planning: aspects of learning, themes, competences and dimensions.

DFE – Department for Education, formerly the Department of Education and Science (DES).

Differentiation – planning of pupils' work to take account of differences in the abilities, aptitudes and needs of individual pupils. Also used in the context of assessment where differentiation by task and by outcome are used to assess what pupils know, understand and can do.

End of key stage statements (EKSS) – more general than **SoA,** these are statutory statements representing the knowledge, skills and understanding which pupils of different abilities and maturities can be expected to achieve by the end of the key stage in question.

ERA – *Education Reform Act 1988* (HMSO, 1989).

Foundation subjects – the subjects of the National Curriculum, as set out in Section 3 of **ERA:** mathematics, science, English, Welsh, technology, history, geography, art, music and physical education and, for secondary-age pupils, a modern foreign language. (The term foundation subjects refers to both core and other foundation subjects.)

Full course – a National Curriculum course which is based on all the **ATs** and **PoS** of a particular subject order.

General Certificate of Secondary Secondary Education (GCSE) – introduced in 1988 to replace the former General Certificate of Education (GCE) and the Certificate of Secondary Education (CSE). This is currently the main form of assessment at the end of **KS4.**

Key stages (KS) – the periods in each pupil's education to which the elements of the National Curriculum apply. There are four key stages, normally related to the age of the majority of pupils in a teaching group. They are: beginning of compulsory education to 7, 7–11, 11–14 and 14 to end of compulsory education.

Levels of attainment – the 10 different levels of attainment defined within each **AT,** reflecting differences in ability and in progress, normally according to age. Art, music and physical education do not have levels or **SoA.**

Modifications and disapplications – terms used to describe various arrangements for lifting part or all of the National Curriculum requirements for individuals, schools, or any other grouping specified by the Secretaries of State.

National Curriculum (NC) – the core and other foundation subjects and their associated **ATs, PoS** and **assessment arrangements**.

National tasks and tests – externally set but internally assessed tasks and tests used at or near the end of the key stage.

NCC – National Curriculum Council

Non-statutory examples – examples given in italics in the Order which are non-statutory and serve to illustrate **SoA, end of key stage statements** or aspects of the **PoS.**

Non-statutory guidance (NSG) – guidance produced by **NCC** and **CCW** to accompany the statutory Order for each National Curriculum subject. NSG goes in the ringbinder with the Order but has no statutory force.

Programmes of study (PoS) – the matters, skills and processes which must be taught to pupils during each key stage in order for them to meet the objectives set out in **ATs.**

Progression	– building systematically on pupils' knowledge, concepts, skills and attitudes to ensure development of their capabilities over a period of time.
Reporting ages	– the four points at which performance is subject to formal reported assessment in relation to National Curriculum levels or end of key stage statements. Also known as key ages or assessment ages, these are at or near the end of each key stage, when most pupils are likely to be 7, 11, 14 and 16, respectively.
SCAA	– School Curriculum and Assessment Authority, see page 10.
School where Welsh is taught	– a school or part of a school where, in relation to the first year of the relevant key stage referred to, Welsh has been taught as a curriculum subject in either school year 1987–88 or 1988–89.
SEAC	– School Examinations and Assessment Council.
Short course	– a National Curriculum course defined in a statutory Order. A short course requires about half the teaching time of a full course, and has a reduced **PoS** based on the full course.
Standard assessment tasks	– see **National tasks and tests.**
Statements of attainment (SoA)	– more precise objectives than the broader **ATs**, which are defined within statutory Orders. They are related to one of 10 levels of attainment on a single continuous scale, covering all four key stages. They are not used in art, music or physical education.
Statutory Order	– the legal document (Statutory Instrument) which puts into effect decisions of the Secretaries of State to use powers given to them by Act of Parliament.
Strand	– a sequence of related **SoA** or ideas running through several levels of an **AT** or parts of **PoS.**
Teacher assessment (TA)	– assessment throughout the key stage undertaken by teachers as a normal part of teaching and learning.
TGAT	– Tasks Group on Assessment and Testing. (Set up in July 1987 to advise the Secretaries of State; main report published in December 1987 recommending a 10-level scale for assessment and reporting.)
Transition	– the movement of pupils between classes, teachers and schools.

Welsh-speaking schools – those schools in which more than half the basic curriculum subjects, other than English and Welsh, are taught wholly or partly through the medium of the Welsh language.

Whole Curriculum – the curriculum of a school, incorporating the basic curriculum and all other provisions. See **cross-curricular elements.**

WOED – Welsh Office Education Department.